50
WHISPERS

Poems By
Extraordinary Women

By
ABRIANA JETTÉ

STAY THIRSTY PRESS
An Imprint of Stay Thirsty Publishing

A Division of

STAY THIRSTY MEDIA, INC.

staythirsty.com

Copyright © 2014 by Abriana Jetté
All Rights Reserved

All poems in this book were first published prior to 1923.

For information about permission to reproduce selections from this book, write to info@staythirstymedia.com
Atten: Permissions.

Cover Design: Jason Mathews

Abriana Jetté

50 WHISPERS

Poems By Extraordinary Women

DEDICATION

To these extraordinary women, whose grace and courage never falters, this book is for you.

INTRODUCTION

As I put together this anthology, three mantras resounded in my head: My sisters' words are my words. My sisters' words are my words, so I must do them justice. My sisters' words are my words, so I must choose the words that speak closest to my beliefs.

I share this mantra with you because I believe it is important to understand that I do not intend for this book to reflect a historical reading or academic inquiry of the history of the female, antifeminism, and/or suffragist culture. There are plenty of fine scholars who have already done the research, specified research, on individual poets and years and social constructs that circle back to the power of the female: I encourage you to do that reading. Rather, this is a book designed by a poet, who is also a woman, with the intention of creating a protected space for the dynamic, lyrical, and heart-wrenching female voices of the past to mingle together.

For many, womanhood is an inescapable myth, a lifetime of predetermined emotions and values and categories in which many do not fit: girlhood, sisterhood, motherhood. These poems speak to each other in that they fill the others' grooves; the way they move on the page and in the mouth echoes the sentiments of the past to pave the sounds of the future. The individual history of each one of these women is made possible because of the ones who came prior, thus they are intertwined. Some of these women, like Gertrude Stein, Emily Dickinson, or H.D. are still celebrated in literary circles today. Others like Lady Kasa or Helen Gray Cone have hid in the shadows: this is their place to shine. In a way, this anthology was created so that these exquisite and already intertwined deserving female poets finally had a safe haven. In a way, I set off to create a sisterhood.

But this sisterhood was not easy to create. For a long while I sat with these poets and poems scattered about my office searching for a thread. I read through them and jotted corresponding notes in the margins. I knew from the start setting off to arrange these poems chronologically would be horribly boring. I knew that worldwide, records spanning decades upon decades exist without the whisper of a woman's verse. This is a heartbreaking fact. In the pages of our global history, women hardly exist. Common sense allows one to understand that surely they existed--societies flourished, didn't they? As in, became populated? Scientifically speaking women, just as men, are a necessity for the continuation of human life.

Scholars, many of them male, will answer in response to this conundrum that *certain avenues were just not made available to women*, or that in later centuries *they enjoyed keeping to the house and children*; some readers and listeners will shake their heads in agreement, shrugging to the stereotype: that's just the way it was.

I imagine the voices of these women were not shunned over night. But when, finally, the last woman stood up for her right to write down her feelings, and our graceful, intuitive, empathetic thoughts were forbidden from the record, there were a few good men out there who realized it was wrong. There had to be a son, a brother, maybe even a father, with a decent set of ethics because he was raised by a good woman who taught him better: a good mother.

Yes, forbidden. Not scrapped, nor erased. Forbidden, unlawful.

Why would a woman be forbidden to write? What is the harm in a poem?

Disguised within the passions of literature is the history of the time. Today, there are still a great number of countries whose leaders prohibit women the same freedoms as men. As deeply as we feel the arts, writing, poetry, singing, and dancing, and all such personal joys are innately within us, they are not considered world-wide natural freedoms. The struggles of these women were in the bow of my mind, sailing with me as I searched for the voices to fill these pages.

Indeed, many of the poems in this anthology can be read as historical fictions in verse, specifically, and purposefully, those in HER STORY AS HISTORY, which features poetry by Queen Elizabeth I, Amy Lowell, Phillis Wheatley, and others whose politically charged language and empathetic lyricism provide annals into a literary and economic past. The woes of freedom expressed in Emma Lazarus's sonnet "1492" mirror the tensions of the immigration process still encountered, in New York City and beyond. In truth, it is agonizing to recognize the parallels between the rights women yearned for in our yesteryear and the struggles and stereotypes still present today.

We know there have been good men. We know that Lady Kasa's ex-lover printed twenty-nine of her love poems, eternalizing her voice. We know that Christina Rossetti's father taught her fairy-tales and poetry, encouraging her to use her mind. And I know that I have not set off to bash a gender, rather to unite one. Peppered throughout the anthology, and the entire focus of SISTERHOOD, are poems that praise the sublime connection of female friendship.

This anthology offers diligent credit to the good men in LOVE SONGS--Today, Anne Bradstreet's "To my Dear Loving Husband" survives vigorously in countless wedding ceremonies across the United States: a semantic manifestation of marital bliss. It is impossible not to be swooned by the passionate fervor and dedication Bradstreet had for her partner. Reading her, one understands commitment.

Though it is unusual for our society to embrace it (the hyperbolic caricature of a woman on television is often a gossip, a harlot, deceitful, or filled with pride/jealousy), female friendship is a crucial factor in helping to discover the inner self. This collection begins in praise of friendship, releasing the positive, intelligent energy of our sisters. Whether for historical analysis or for amusement, eroticized readings of hetero-social poetry often conclude with the same thesis: same-sex-adoration is natural. It is okay to feel love for your beautiful friend who made you laugh in the garden. If that's not love, what is?

Certainly it is safe to say that it is not the good that draws us to poetry, but revelation. Poetry allows insight into those chaotic, maddening moments, those moments when a guilt-ridden, hopeless, gut-wrenching pit of a feeling envelops the being; it offers solace on those frightening, lonely days. Poetry tells us these days are normal; these days happen. The IN BETWEEN memorializes such rejected and tormented spirits, and will offer solace to anyone feeling a little less than satisfied with the world.

MOREOVER, THE MOON, the final section of this anthology, pays tribute to the definitive symbol of the feminine spirit, our one and only moon, the ultimate symbol of feminine prowess.

I have tried my hardest to assimilate a wide variety of voices in this collection, in respect to era, literary genre, and global perspective. Because of this, I've had to search for poetry from other languages, languages I don't fluently or naturally speak, like ancient Greek or Japanese. The art of literary translation is one I greatly admire. For the purpose of this anthology, I followed these three rules of translation:

1. The poet is my sister.

2. I must retain my sister's intention; I must keep the meaning of her poem.

3. My translation, as hard as it will try, will never be identical to the original.

With each new poem a translator must sacrifice something, choosing and rendering the most useful aspects of the original which best fit the translator's particular voice. I do not claim to be an expert on these particular poets or on the art of translation, but I do know that my mission, my mantra, was to share my sisters' words as if they were my words. I hope I have honored them. Translation takes one culture's poetry and puts it into another. What else is so miraculous?

Every poem in here is a poem of a culture: they are all voices of the past. The poems in this anthology have been singing for over one hundred years. Listen to them. Hear them. Here is to one hundred more.

Abriana Jetté
Brooklyn, NY

TABLE OF CONTENTS

(i)
SISTERHOOD (25)

Anne Kingsmill Finch ... *Friendship Between Ephelia And Ardelia* (27)

Lady Mary Chudleigh ... *To the Ladies* (29)

Emily Dickinson ... *One Sister Have I in our House* (31)

Katherine Phillips ... *Orinda To Lucasia Parting October 1661 At London* (33)

H.D. ... *Gertrude Stein* (37)

Ann Taylor ... *About the Little Girl that Beat Her Sister* (39)

Sappho ... *To Erinna* (41)

(ii)
THE FALLEN & THE FORGIVEN (43)

Sumangalamata ... *Women Well Set Free* (47)

Christina Rossetti ... *A Daughter of Eve* (49)

Aphra Behn ... *The Willing Mistress* (51)

Louise Labe ... *I Live, I Die, I Burn, I Drown* (53)

Lady Kasa ... *Untitled* (55)

H.D. ... *Leda* (57)

Elizabeth Barrett Browning ... *Mother and Poet* (59)

Phillis Wheatley ... *A Funeral Poem on the Death of C.E. -- an infant aged twelve months* (65)

(iii)
HER STORY AS HISTORY (69)

Lucy Terry (Prince) ... *Bars Fight* (71)

Anne Bradstreet ... *Verses on the Burning of Our House, July 18, 1666* (73)

Queen Elizabeth I ... *Written on a Wall at Woodstock* (77)

Anna Laetitia Barbauld ... *The Rights of Woman* (79)

Phillis Wheatley ... *To The Right Honourable William, Earl Of Dartmouth, His Majesty's Principal Secretary Of The State For North-America* (81)

Amy Lowell ... *1777* (83)

Isabella Whitney ... *from The Manner of Her Will...* (91)

Emma Lazarus ... *1492* (97)

(iv)
THE IN BETWEEN (99)

Emily Brontë ... *Spellbound* (101)

Christina Rossetti ... *Dream Land* (103)

Mary Darby Robinson ... *Sonnet XXI: Why Do I Live* (105)

Sara Teasdale ... *House of Dreams* (107)

Jane Austen ... *Ode to Pity* (109)

Emily Dickinson ... *We Dream -- it is Good we are Dreaming* (111)

Amy Lowell ... *Grotesque* (113)

Anne Kingsmill Finch ... *To Death* (115)

(v)
MOTHER - NATURE - RAIN (117)

Li Quingzhau Ci... *Huan Xi Sha* (119)

Helen Gray Cone ... *In Winter, With the Book We Read in Spring* (121)

H.D. ... *Garden* (123)

Emily Dickinson ... *Nature, the Gentlest Mother* (125)

Ella Wheeler Wilcox ... *Bleak Weather* (127)

Anne Kingsmill Finch ... *The Tree* (129)

Emily Brontë ... *High waving heather, 'neath stormy blasts bending* (131)

(vi)
LOVE SONGS (133)

Mina Loy ... *Love Songs* (135)

Anne Bradstreet ... *To My Dear Loving Husband* (137)

Sappho ... *Epithalamion* (139)

Emma Lazarus ... *Venus of the Louvre* (141)

Katherine Phillips ... *Against Love* (143)

Mary Darby Robinson ... *Stanzas to Love* (145)

(vii)
MOREOVER, THE MOON (147)

Mina Loy ... *Moreover, The Moon –* (149)

Sappho ... *Moon and Stars* (151)

Elizabeth Barrett Browning ... *A Sea-side Walk* (153)

Mary Darby Robinson ... *Ode to the Moon* (155)

Felicia Dorothea Hemans ... *Moon-Light* (159)

Gertrude Stein ... *A Light in the Moon* (161)

ABOUT THE AUTHOR (165)

SISTERHOOD

Walking with a friend in the dark is better than walking alone in the light.
-Helen Keller

Friendship (noun):
(1) an emotional attachment of affection or regard felt for another
(2) one who offers supports.

What better way to begin our sojourn into the past than with supportive and encouraging incantations from sister to sister. The simple purpose of this section is to promote positivity within feminine culture. As a whole, we must step away from beauty-bashing or fat-shaming because what matters most is the way we make one another feel. If woman put one another down because of minuscule frivolities, we subconsciously give the world permission to put us down, too. Indeed, the power of friendship is that it makes one feel that anything is possible. Supportive friends are the key to success.

The definition of friendship is ambiguous, specifically when understanding the boundaries of its emotional attachment. Some of these poems, for some readers, may push beyond the conventional limit of friendship, especially Sappho's "To Erinna", which is more a profession of desire than a benediction of friendship. Still, the adoration and support for the other is ever-present. Even our very first poem by Anne Kingsmill Finch confesses that the truest love of all is the love shared between two female friends.

ANNE KINGSMILL FINCH
1661-1720

Daughter of Sir William Kingsmill, Anne Kingsmill Finch wrote often about her depression and fervor for social equality amongst the sexes. In the following poem, Finch imagines a dialogue over the definition of ideal love between two friends. When their examples become too literary or too ambiguous, they realize the best example of friendship they can come up with is the type they share with one another. The rhyming couplets of the poem further enhance the harmonious bond that the two women share. In all, our first poem reveals to readers the mighty bond of sisterhood.

Friendship Between Ephelia And Ardelia

Eph. What Friendship is, Ardelia shew.
Ard. 'Tis to love, as I love You.
Eph. This Account, so short (tho' kind)
     Suits not my enquiring Mind.
     Therefore farther now repeat;
     What is Friendship when complete?
Ard. 'Tis to share all Joy and Grief;
     'Tis to lend all due Relief

      From the Tongue, the Heart, the Hand;
      'Tis to mortgage House and Land;
      For a Friend be sold a Slave;
      'Tis to die upon a Grave,
      If a Friend therein do lie.
Eph. This indeed, tho' carry'd high,
      This, tho' more than e'er was done
      Underneath the rolling Sun,
      This has all been said before.
      Can Ardelia say no more?
Ard. Words indeed no more can shew:
      But 'tis to love, as I love you.

LADY MARY CHUDLEIGH
1656-1710

Born to Richard Lee, Lady Mary Chudleigh read widely as a child, and was self-educated in theology, philosophy, and art. In the following anthem against marriages of convenience, Lady Mary Chudleigh addresses the relinquishment of the self that was expected of a wife. Once married, a woman was presumed to behave "like a mute", Chudleigh describes, who "fears her husband as a God." Particularly interesting to me is the phrase "which nothing, nothing can divide" because it challenges the romantic idiom of "nothing can break our love" to signal the chains that bound the wife to her husband. Legally, she had no right to leave him. The beauty in the poem belongs to its universal anger. In sharing her fit of passion, Lady Mary Chudleigh reminds all women who suffer from some form of submission that they are not alone.

To the Ladies

Wife and servant are the same,
But only differ in the name:

For when that fatal knot is ty'd,
Which nothing, nothing can divide:
When she the word obey has said,
And man by law supreme has made,
Then all that's kind is laid aside,
And nothing left but state and pride:
Fierce as an eastern prince he grows,
And all his innate rigour shows:
Then but to look, to laugh, or speak,
Will the nuptial contract break.
Like mutes, she signs alone must make,
And never any freedom take:
But still be govern'd by a nod,
And fear her husband as a God:
Him still must serve, him still obey,
And nothing act, and nothing say,
But what her haughty lord thinks fit,
Who with the power, has all the wit.
Then shun, oh ! shun that wretched state,
And all the fawning flatt'rers hate:
Value yourselves, and men despise:
You must be proud, if you'll be wise.

EMILY DICKINSON
1830-1886

Born into an affluent family in Amherst, Massachusetts, Emily Dickinson is one of America's most beloved poets. Her mysteriousness and insular lifestyle add to her popularity: she is well known for her reclusive nature. The following poem offers a rare glimpse of the poet's friendship with her sister-in-law, Sue, who, before marriage, was a dear friend to the poet. On one hand, the poem embraces the legal notion that a sister-in-law is a true part of the family, while on the other, the arduous language and warm temperament confessed for Sue raises eyebrows, hinting towards the rhetoric of erotic love.

One Sister Have I in our House

One Sister have I in our house -
And one a hedge away.
There's only one recorded,
But both belong to me.

One came the way that I came -

And wore my past year's gown -
The other as a bird her nest,
Builded our hearts among.

She did not sing as we did -
It was a different tune -
Herself to her a Music
As Bumble-bee of June.

Today is far from Childhood -
But up and down the hills
I held her hand the tighter -
Which shortened all the miles -

And still her hum
The years among,
Deceives the Butterfly;
Still in her Eye
The Violets lie
Mouldered this many May.

I spilt the dew -
But took the morn, -
I chose this single star
From out the wide night's numbers -

Sue - forevermore!

KATHERINE PHILLIPS
1632-1664

Legend has it that Katherine Phillips read the Bible in its entirety by the time she was five years young. Phillips, who helped eternalize the literary trope of an *Orinda*, the stock character of an elderly widow fallen to the tender mercies of love, yearned for her readers to understand that love was more than passion and earthly pleasures. This detailed portrait of two friends parting testifies to the power of female friendship, a type of friendship known to persevere regardless of great distances and lengthy periods of time.

Orinda To Lucasia Parting October 1661 At London

Adieu dear object of my Love's excess,
And with thee all my hopes of happiness,
With the same fervent and unchanged heart
Which did it's whole self once to thee impart,
(And which though fortune has so sorely bruis'd,
Would suffer more, to be from this excus'd)
I to resign thy dear Converse submit,
Since I can neither keep, nor merit it.
Thou hast too long to me confined been,
Who ruine am without, passion within.
My mind is sunk below thy tenderness,

And my condition does deserve it less;
I'm so entangl'd and so lost a thing
By all the shocks my daily sorrow bring,
That would'st thou for thy old Orinda call
Thou hardly could'st unravel her at all.
And should I thy clear fortunes interline
With the incessant miseries of mine?
No, no, I never lov'd at such a rate
To tye thee to the rigours of my fate,
As from my obligations thou art free,
Sure thou shalt be so from my Injury,
Though every other worthiness I miss,
Yet I'le at least be generous in this.
I'd rather perish without sigh or groan,
Then thou shoul'dst be condemn'd to give me one;
Nay in my soul I rather could allow
Friendship should be a sufferer, then thou;
Go then, since my sad heart has set thee free,
Let all the loads and chains remain on me.
Though I be left the prey of sea and wind,
Thou being happy wilt in that be kind;
Nor shall I my undoing much deplore,
Since thou art safe, whom I must value more.
Oh! mayst thou ever be so, and as free
From all ills else, as from my company,
And may the torments thou hast had from it
Be all that heaven will to thy life permit.
And that they may thy vertue service do,
Mayest thou be able to forgive them too:
But though I must this sharp submission learn,
I cannot yet unwish thy dear concern.
Not one new comfort I expect to see,
I quit my Joy, hope, life, and all but thee;
Nor seek I thence ought that may discompose

That mind where so serene a goodness grows.
I ask no inconvenient kindness now,
To move thy passion, or to cloud thy brow;
And thou wilt satisfie my boldest plea
By some few soft remembrances of me,
Which may present thee with this candid thought,
I meant not all the troubles that I brought.
Own not what Passion rules, and Fate does crush,
But wish thou couldst have don't without a blush,
And that I had been, ere it was too late,
Either more worthy, or more fortunate.
Ah who can love the thing they cannot prize?
But thou mayst pity though thou dost despise.
Yet I should think that pity bought too dear,
If it should cost those precious Eyes a tear.

Oh may no minutes trouble, thee possess,
But to endear the next hours happiness;
And maist thou when thou art from me remov'd,
Be better pleas'd, but never worse belov'd:
Oh pardon me for pow'ring out my woes
In Rhime now, that I dare not do't in Prose.
For I must lose whatever is call'd dear,
And thy assistance all that loss to bear,
And have more cause than ere I had before,
To fear that I shall never see thee more.

H.D. (Hilda Doolittle)
1886-1961

When Hilda Doolittle moved to London in 1911, she took up the pen name H.D. and became one of the foremost prominent figures of the Imagist movement. In the following poem, she praises fellow poet Gertrude Stein by juxtaposing her craft to that of legendary Physicist and Chemist, Marie Curie, who is most famous for being the first woman to win the Nobel Peace Prize amongst her many other accolades. In calling upon the spirit of another inspirational female leader, H.D. subconsciously preaches the message that praising one another, rather than competing with one another, encourages creativity, productivity, and positivity amongst women.

Gertrude Stein

Curie
of the laboratory
of vocabulary
she crushed
the tonnage
of consciousness
congealed to phrases
to extract
a radium of the word

ANN TAYLOR
1782-1866

From birth, Ann Taylor was introduced to the craft of poetry, and she was able to make a career of critiquing the art later on in her life. Seemingly playful, her children's poetry tends to reveal the dark history of the acquiescence of the little girl. The theme of the young girl behaving like a proper lady is directly addressed in the following poem. The poem's rhyme scheme add to the illusion of simplicity, but the poem is complicated in terms of its forward announcement of how "shocking" it is to see such anger in an innocent child. The unknown relationship between the speaker, little girl, and sister add an extra layer of tension to the poem.

About the Little Girl that Beat Her Sister

Go, go, my naughty girl, and kiss
Your little sister dear;
I must not have such things as this,
And noisy quarrels here.

What! little children scratch and fight,
That ought to be so mild;

Oh! Mary, it's a shocking sight
To see an angry child.

I can't imagine, for my part,
The reason for your folly;
She did not do you any hurt
By playing with your dolly.

See, see, the little tears that run
Fast from her watery eye:
Come, my sweet innocent, have done,
'Twill do no good to cry.

Go, Mary, wipe her tears away,
And make it up with kisses:
And never turn a pretty play
To such a pet as this is.

SAPPHO
630/612-570 BC

Translators all over the globe flock Sappho's succinct verse. Though little is factually known of her life, we can say assuredly that Sappho was born on the island of Lesbos, and that the Alexandrians considered her one of the best nine lyric poets. The sharp presentation of emotion and image in her poetry is just one contribution to her lasting power. In the following fragment, Sappho surrenders to her passions for her fair friend and fellow poet, Erinna. In my translation, I attempted to preserve the Sapphic stanza, a form of poetry that, in its barest state, is made of four line stanzas in which the first three lines carry eleven syllables and the last line is composed of five syllables.

To Erinna

Haughtier than you, my fair Erinna, I
have never met another maiden. Such
thoughtlessness towards my passion is an insult
to Aphrodite.
One day the dart of desire will strike your
heart: then you'll know love's pain. Then you'll suffer for

us both. Keep the riches I gave you: fabric
from Phocea for
your lap, perfumed leathers for your feet, the rich
velvety Babylonian cream and frames
mounted in gold and ivory to honor
the Goddess. For her
delight I send sacrificial flames, sacred
mists of devotion to please her spirit. And
during that hour I let fall all thoughts of
your breasts and my mouth.

THE FALLEN & THE FORGIVEN

What is the use of a violent kind of delightfulness if there is no pleasure in not getting tired of it?
-Gertrude Stein

There is a myth that still exists in contemporary cultures which preaches the belief that women are inferior to men. I know, it sounds absurd, but its origins are deeply rooted in the interpretation of the creation story during which Eve is created after, therefor other and below, Adam. My commentary here should not be mistaken as an argument over the validity of the myth of creation, rather a commentary on it. After Eve, Adam's play-mate, is seduced by the serpent, the world needs saving: for many Christians, the savior is found in their father, Jesus Christ. From this narrative two stereotypes have emerged, and as if out of Pandora's Box, have never been able to be put away. These widely held misconceptions subliminally or blatantly appear in all forms of literature, music, and pop culture: a woman is either a priestess, saved, pure and innocent, putting others before her and blindly accepting the flaws of those she loves, or she can be stained, tainted, seductive, the devil, powerful: like a man.

You don't need to agree with me, but consider Lady Mary Chudleigh's supposition that a wife is synonymous to a slave. The men in Chudleigh's time openly supported the submission of the female; legally, men were superior. Frighteningly, this was not just an idea, it was a law. Caroline Norton summarizes the rights of a wife in 19th century Britain perfectly in *A Letter to the Queen on Lord Chancellor Cranworth's Marriage and Divorce Bill* (1854), in which she states, "in short, as her husband, he has the right to all that is hers; as his wife she has no right to anything that is his." In the 19th century, wide circulation of the image of "the Angel in the House" administered the belief that an ideal woman carried a submissive and malleable identity. Virginia Woolf famously believed it was the female writer's duty to "kill the angel in the house."

There is no room for the belief of inferior sexes in poetry. Poetry suspends any preconceived gender specified notions. The female poet can adopt the voice of a man, of a star, or of a storm cloud brewing; the male poet may take over the voice of a young girl, or Queen, or a boat traveling the open sea. Indeed, poetry may offer the only true voice for those who feel they do not conform to any specified gender. What matters to the poem, to the poet, and to the reader are the words, the form, the incantatory rhythms, how it makes the reader feel, and what desires it stirs.

The following poems approach this paradox of womanhood and battle the ideas of temptation, forgiveness, and freedom.

SUMANGALAMATA
600BC (?)

It is frightening to imagine history without Sumangalamata, wife of a hat-maker in ancient India. She is a pioneer. Without her it isn't far-fetched to say that the Brontë's and Phillip's of the world would never have been able to share their thoughts on the oppressive nature of marriage and the chauvinistic, dominating attitude of the patriarch. Sumangalamata lived as a Buddhist priestess and writer, but she is most revered for successfully divorcing her husband, an almost impossible task in antiquated India. Imagine the difficulty, imagine her persuasiveness. The following poem praises female freedom and paves the way for all women to release themselves from the unjustified maltreatment of despotic husbands.

Women Well Set Free

At last well set free I am!
I am a woman well set free!
Bound no more to the kitchen
stains, scrubbing the pots and pans and

tied no more to that empty man
who braided the shade with his hands.
At last I hold no more
anger, at last my hunger has waned.
I sit under my own shade.
I claim my own tree.
At last I am serene!

CHRISTINA ROSSETTI
1830-1894

Rossetti's words have served as the source of inspiration for writers like Elizabeth Jennings, Virginia Woolf, and J.K. Rowling. Her mother and father (political exile and poet Gabriel Rossetti) homeschooled their daughter, and she was encouraged to write formal poetry and short stories throughout her childhood. Though briefly engaged, Rossetti was never married; rather than leave the world a legacy of children, she left a legacy of powerful poetry. The following poem describes the inner workings of the mind when controlled by something other than rational thinking. The preconceived ideals of womanhood addressed in the poem, rooted in the inferiority and unworthiness of the female species, begin with its title.

A Daughter of Eve

A fool I was to sleep at noon,
    And wake when night is chilly
Beneath the comfortless cold moon;
A fool to pluck my rose too soon,
    A fool to snap my lily.

My garden-plot I have not kept;
    Faded and all-forsaken,
I weep as I have never wept:
Oh it was summer when I slept,
    It's winter now I waken.

Talk what you please of future spring
    And sun-warm'd sweet to-morrow:—
Stripp'd bare of hope and everything,
No more to laugh, no more to sing,
    I sit alone with sorrow.

APHRA BEHN
1640-1689

Of Aphra Behn little is known, and she isn't as widely read as one might expect, especially considering the bold, sensual nature of her work. She was employed as a spy in the Netherlands for the British Royal family, but after struggling with poverty, she focused her energy on her writing, and successfully published over a dozen plays and countless poems. The following poem is a startling scene of deceit and submission to temptation. It is difficult now, considering the oversexualized advertisements that bombard most media outlets, to imagine how radical Behn's verse would have been for her day. To say the least, this is the polar opposite of the angel in the house. This is the temptress in the garden.

The Willing Mistress

Amyntas led me to a Grove,
Where all the Trees did shade us;
The Sun it self, though it had Strove,
It could not have betray'd us:
The place secur'd from humane Eyes,
No other fear allows,

But when the Winds that gently rise,
Doe Kiss the yielding Boughs.

Down there we satt upon the Moss,
And did begin to play
A Thousand Amorous Tricks, to pass
The heat of all the day.
A many Kisses he did give:
And I return'd the same
Which made me willing to receive
That which I dare not name.
His Charming Eyes no Aid requir'd
To tell their softning Tale;
On her that was already fir'd,
'Twas Easy to prevaile.
He did but Kiss and Clasp me round,
Whilst those his thoughts Exprest:
And lay'd me gently on the Ground:
Ah who can guess the rest?

LOUISE LABE
1520/25-1566

Descended from a family of rope-makers, Louise Labe was born into a moment in history when the themes and ideas of the Italian renaissance strongly influenced the French. Because of these newly constituted creative freedoms, she was able to establish herself as a celebrated poet, regardless of her ignoble family. Her work centers on the courageous voice of a woman, and her legend lends itself to setting the stones for the suffragist movement. Her ability to weave social issues with the turmoil of internal consciousness is just one demonstration of the eternity of her poetic voice. The following poem, written in unrhymed quatrains, handles the inconsistencies of human existence as it boldly confronts the cyclical nature of emotional instability that is a woman's life.

I Live, I Die, I Burn, I Drown

I live, I die, I burn, I drown
I endure at once chill and cold
Life is at once too soft and too hard
I have sore troubles mingled with joys

Suddenly I laugh and at the same time cry
And in pleasure many a grief endure
My happiness wanes and yet it lasts unchanged
All at once I dry up and grow green

Thus I suffer love's inconstancies
And when I think the pain is most intense
Without thinking, it is gone again.

Then when I feel my joys certain
And my hour of greatest delight arrived
I find my pain beginning all over once again.

LADY KASA
8th Century

Whatever scholars know about Lady Kasa is derived from the collection of love poems, which she gave to her former lover, Yakamochi. Yakamochi was a prominent writer of the time, and published twenty-nine of Lady Kasa's poems in Man'yōshū. Because of him, we have not lost her. The wrenching simplicity of the following poem illustrates the madness of love-sickness and the importance of dreams: two poetic tropes perfect for intertwining images of a tempted woman. In my translation, I found the paratactic manipulation of breath most important to conserve.

Untitled

I dreamt I touched
the sword to my chest.
What could it mean?
It means I will see you soon.

H.D. (Hilda Doolittle)
1886-1961

Friends with Ezra Pound and Sigmund Freud, H.D.'s poetry is unapologetic, dangerous, chaotic, and at times astonishing. She was a patient of the grandfather of psychology, and because she underwent this psychological practice she was better able to search deep into her subconscious and scoop out the words and themes that most shook her soul. In the following poem, she boldly rewrites the myth of Leda, who was raped by Zeus disguised as a swan. Consequently, Leda birthed Helen of Troy, the face that launched a thousand ships. H.D.'s imagistic use of color and liquidy images transform the antiquated story into a living, contemporary tale.

Leda

Where the slow river
meets the tide,
a red swan lifts red wings
and darker beak,
and underneath the purple down
of his soft breast

uncurls his coral feet.

Through the deep purple
of the dying heat
of sun and mist,
the level ray of sun-beam
has caressed
the lily with dark breast,
and flecked with richer gold
its golden crest.

Where the slow lifting
of the tide,
floats into the river
and slowly drifts
among the reeds,
and lifts the yellow flags,
he floats
where tide and river meet.

Ah kingly kiss --
no more regret
nor old deep memories
to mar the bliss;
where the low sedge is thick,
the gold day-lily
outspreads and rests
beneath soft fluttering
of red swan wings
and the warm quivering
of the red swan's breast.

ELIZABETH BARRETT BROWNING
1806-1861

She was the eldest of twelve children in a strict religious household. Elizabeth Barrett Browning lived a life immersed in frailty, sickness, and letters. Nonetheless, she gained notoriety as one of the most popular Victorian poets, especially amongst the upper classes. In fact, in many literary circles, Browning was considered an inimitable poet. It is no doubt that the political turmoil brewing in the middle of the eighteenth and nineteenth century altered the ferocity of her writing. The following poem, which was written during the year of Browning's death, is based off the true story of Laura Savio of Turin's sons, who died a short time after one another. It attempts to bring order to death through its organization and repetition. Most of all, the poem recognizes that for some women there is a type of pain, like the pain of burying two sons, that is inconsolable.

Mother and Poet

I.
Dead ! One of them shot by the sea in the east,

And one of them shot in the west by the sea.
Dead ! both my boys ! When you sit at the feast
And are wanting a great song for Italy free,
Let none look at me !

II.
Yet I was a poetess only last year,
And good at my art, for a woman, men said ;
But this woman, this, who is agonized here,
-- The east sea and west sea rhyme on in her head
For ever instead.

III.
What art can a woman be good at ? Oh, vain !
What art is she good at, but hurting her breast
With the milk-teeth of babes, and a smile at the pain ?
Ah boys, how you hurt ! you were strong as you pressed,
And I proud, by that test.

IV.
What art's for a woman ? To hold on her knees
Both darlings ! to feel all their arms round her throat,
Cling, strangle a little ! to sew by degrees
And 'broider the long-clothes and neat little coat ;
To dream and to doat.

V.
To teach them ... It stings there ! I made them indeed
Speak plain the word country. I taught them, no doubt,
That a country's a thing men should die for at need.
I prated of liberty, rights, and about
The tyrant cast out.

VI.

And when their eyes flashed ... O my beautiful eyes ! ...
I exulted ; nay, let them go forth at the wheels
Of the guns, and denied not. But then the surprise
When one sits quite alone ! Then one weeps, then one kneels !
God, how the house feels !

VII.
At first, happy news came, in gay letters moiled
With my kisses, -- of camp-life and glory, and how
They both loved me ; and, soon coming home to be spoiled
In return would fan off every fly from my brow
With their green laurel-bough.

VIII.
Then was triumph at Turin : `Ancona was free !'
And some one came out of the cheers in the street,
With a face pale as stone, to say something to me.
My Guido was dead ! I fell down at his feet,
While they cheered in the street.

IX.
I bore it ; friends soothed me ; my grief looked sublime
As the ransom of Italy. One boy remained
To be leant on and walked with, recalling the time
When the first grew immortal, while both of us strained
To the height he had gained.

X.
And letters still came, shorter, sadder, more strong,
Writ now but in one hand, `I was not to faint, --
One loved me for two -- would be with me ere long :
And Viva l' Italia ! -- he died for, our saint,
Who forbids our complaint."

XI.
My Nanni would add, `he was safe, and aware
Of a presence that turned off the balls, -- was imprest
It was Guido himself, who knew what I could bear,
And how 'twas impossible, quite dispossessed,
To live on for the rest."

XII.
On which, without pause, up the telegraph line
Swept smoothly the next news from Gaeta : -- Shot.
Tell his mother. Ah, ah, ` his, ' ` their ' mother, -- not ` mine, '
No voice says "My mother" again to me. What !
You think Guido forgot ?

XIII.
Are souls straight so happy that, dizzy with Heaven,
They drop earth's affections, conceive not of woe ?
I think not. Themselves were too lately forgiven
Through that Love and Sorrow which reconciled so
The Above and Below.

XIV.
O Christ of the five wounds, who look'dst through the dark
To the face of thy mother ! consider, I pray,
How we common mothers stand desolate, mark,
Whose sons, not being Christs, die with eyes turned away,
And no last word to say !

XV.
Both boys dead ? but that's out of nature. We all
Have been patriots, yet each house must always keep one.
'Twere imbecile, hewing out roads to a wall ;
And, when Italy 's made, for what end is it done

If we have not a son ?

XVI.
Ah, ah, ah ! when Gaeta's taken, what then ?
When the fair wicked queen sits no more at her sport
Of the fire-balls of death crashing souls out of men ?
When the guns of Cavalli with final retort
Have cut the game short ?

XVII.
When Venice and Rome keep their new jubilee,
When your flag takes all heaven for its white, green, and red,
When you have your country from mountain to sea,
When King Victor has Italy's crown on his head,
(And I have my Dead) --

XVIII.
What then ? Do not mock me. Ah, ring your bells low,
And burn your lights faintly ! My country is there,
Above the star pricked by the last peak of snow :
My Italy 's there, with my brave civic Pair,
To disfranchise despair !

XIX.
Forgive me. Some women bear children in strength,
And bite back the cry of their pain in self-scorn ;
But the birth-pangs of nations will wring us at length
Into wail such as this -- and we sit on forlorn
When the man-child is born.

XX.
Dead ! One of them shot by the sea in the east,
And one of them shot in the west by the sea.
Both ! both my boys ! If in keeping the feast

You want a great song for your Italy free,
Let none look at me !

PHILLIS WHEATLEY
1753-1784

The unfortunate lack of documentation of Phillis Wheatley's origin and date of birth has left scholars only to speculate her upbringing. We believe she was born in West Africa before she was captured and carried over on a slave ship named *The Phillis*, which sailed to Boston. Her masters granted her the name Phillis because of this. Wheatley, who survived slavery only to suffer through poverty, buried two infant children. The nature of the following poem addresses the dreaded act with a tactile sense of empathy and control of narrative.

A Funeral Poem on the Death of C.E.
--an infant aged twelve months

Through airy roads he wings his instant flight
To purer regions of celestial light;
Enlarg'd he sees unnumber'd systems roll,
Beneath him sees the universal whole,
Planets on planets run their destin'd round,
And circling wonders fill the vast profound.
Th' ethereal now, and now th' empyreal skies
With growing splendors strike his wond'ring eyes:
The angels view him with delight unknown,
Press his soft hand, and seat him on his throne;

Then smilling thus: "To this divine abode,
"The seat of saints, of seraphs, and of God,
"Thrice welcome thou." The raptur'd babe replies,
"Thanks to my God, who snatch'd me to the skies,
"E'er vice triumphant had possess'd my heart,
"E'er yet the tempter had beguil'd my heart,
"E'er yet on sin's base actions I was bent,
"E'er yet I knew temptation's dire intent;
"E'er yet the lash for horrid crimes I felt,
"E'er vanity had led my way to guilt,
"But, soon arriv'd at my celestial goal,
"Full glories rush on my expanding soul."
Joyful he spoke: exulting cherubs round
Clapt their glad wings, the heav'nly vaults resound.
Say, parents, why this unavailing moan?
Why heave your pensive bosoms with the groan?
To Charles, the happy subject of my song,
A brighter world, and nobler strains belong.
Say would you tear him from the realms above

By thoughtless wishes, and prepost'rous love?
Doth his felicity increase your pain?
Or could you welcome to this world again
The heir of bliss? with a superior air
Methinks he answers with a smile severe,
"Thrones and dominions cannot tempt me there."

But still you cry, "Can we the sigh forbear,
"And still and still must we not pour the tear?
"Our only hope, more dear than vital breath,
"Twelve moons revolv'd, becomes the prey of death;

"Delightful infant, nightly visions give
"Thee to our arms, and we with joy receive,

"We fain would clasp the Phantom to our breast,
"The Phantom flies, and leaves the soul unblest."

To yon bright regions let your faith ascend,
Prepare to join your dearest infant friend
In pleasures without measure, without end.

HER STORY AS HISTORY

The true worth of a race must be measured by the character of its womanhood.
-Mary McLeod Bethune

Joan of Arc. Queen Elizabeth I. Sacajawae. Marie Curie.

Without Sappho, Lady Kasa, or Marie of France, what would literature be?

How would the world appear today without the brightness of Malala Yousafzai, winner of the 2014 Nobel Peace Prize, and what would a college curriculum be without the Bechdal Test, created by Alison Bechdal, recent winner of the MacArthur Genius Award? It is terrifying to imagine a world without these women, and that's hardly scratching the surface. In fact, all of the women in this anthology have touched the world with their empathetic intelligence and courage. And it is their words we should be remembering, especially during these times of such unnerving political unrest.

When one realizes that women did not achieve universal suffrage until 1928, the urgency within the following poems takes on new force. Until that year, in many westernized countries, a man was still legally allowed to use violence as a disciplinary act towards his wife and/or children. The following poems are first-hand, personal narratives that reflect the tensions of such complicated moments in history.

    I encourage you to read the following section as if it is documentary, as if it is the truth. These are poems inspired by true events, poems told from the voice of powerful, intrepid speakers. Read Anna Letitia Barbauld as an eighteenth century anthropological study. Read Queen Elizabeth's poem as a personalized insight into the boundaries of the law from a woman who would soon control it. These are the poems that remind us that no matter how many decades passed without any publication or acknowledgement of the female, she was there. She was watching. And she was writing it all down.

LUCY TERRY (PRINCE)
1730-1821

Sold into slavery as a child, Lucy Terry Prince wasn't a free woman until 1756; however, the musicality of her words, which drew empathy from listeners, and her ability to tell a story swiftly, delicately, and articulately earned her a reputation as one of the best voices in Vermont. A testament to the power of her storytelling, the following poem survived orally from tavern to dinner table to barn until it was finally published in 1855. It references a true encounter Terry witnessed, the slaughter of her neighbors by the Indians in an area known as the Bars.

Bars Fight

August 'twas the twenty-fifth,
Seventeen hundred forty-six;
The Indians did in ambush lay,
Some very valiant men to slay,
The names of whom I'll not leave out.
Samuel Allen like a hero fout,
And though he was so brave and bold,
His face no more shalt we behold
Eteazer Hawks was killed outright,

Before he had time to fight, -
Before he did the Indians see,
Was shot and killed immediately.
Oliver Amsden he was slain,
Which caused his friends much grief and pain.
Simeon Amsden they found dead,
Not many rods distant from his head.
Adonijah Gillett we do hear
Did lose his life which was so dear.
John Sadler fled across the water,
And thus escaped the dreadful slaughter.
Eunice Allen see the Indians coming,
And hopes to save herself by running,
And had not her petticoats stopped her,
The awful creatures had not catched her,
Nor tommy hawked her on the head,
And left her on the ground for dead.
Young Samuel Allen, Oh lack-a-day!
Was taken and carried to Canada.

ANNE BRADSTREET
1612-1672

Today, Anne Bradstreet holds the title of the first female poet to be published of the British occupied North American colonies, thus paving the way for women writers of the United States. Bradstreet was raised in a fortunate household and her education in history and the humanities was heavily supported. In the following poem, she details the painstaking process of losing her home to a fire with commendable wisdom and distance. In its cinematic unraveling, the poem carries with it the global understanding that is the shock of unexpected loss.

Verses on the Burning of Our House, July 18, 1666

In silent night when rest I took,
For sorrow near I did not look,
I waken'd was with thund'ring noise
And piteous shrieks of dreadful voice.
That fearful sound of 'fire' and 'fire,'
Let no man know is my Desire.
I starting up, the light did spy,
And to my God my heart did cry
To straighten me in my Distress
And not to leave me succourless.

Then coming out, behold a space
The flame consume my dwelling place.
And when I could no longer look,
I blest his grace that gave and took,
That laid my goods now in the dust.
Yea, so it was, and so 'twas just.
It was his own; it was not mine.
Far be it that I should repine,
He might of all justly bereft
But yet sufficient for us left.
When by the Ruins oft I past
My sorrowing eyes aside did cast
And here and there the places spy
Where oft I sate and long did lie.
Here stood that Trunk, and there that chest,
There lay that store I counted best,
My pleasant things in ashes lie
And them behold no more shall I.
Under the roof no guest shall sit,
Nor at thy Table eat a bit.
No pleasant talk shall 'ere be told
Nor things recounted done of old.
No Candle 'ere shall shine in Thee,
Nor bridegroom's voice ere heard shall bee.
In silence ever shalt thou lie.
Adieu, Adieu, All's Vanity.
Then straight I 'gin my heart to chide:
And did thy wealth on earth abide,
Didst fix thy hope on mouldring dust,
The arm of flesh didst make thy trust?
Raise up thy thoughts above the sky
That dunghill mists away may fly.
Thou hast a house on high erect
Fram'd by that mighty Architect,

With glory richly furnished
Stands permanent, though this be fled.
It's purchased and paid for too
By him who hath enough to do.
A price so vast as is unknown,
Yet by his gift is made thine own.
There's wealth enough; I need no more.
Farewell, my pelf; farewell, my store.
The world no longer let me love;
My hope and Treasure lies above.

QUEEN ELIZABETH I
1533-1603

Before she was Queen, she was a disappointment. Henry VIII, Anne Boyelen, and the lot of England hoped to birth a strident young boy to grow as heir of the kingdom. Who could have known her legacy would be one of the most celebrated of royal family's? Of the Queen, many know most about the genre of literature which her reign influenced, for instance, the Elizabethan plays of Edmund Spenser or William Shakespeare. Queen Elizabeth's personal poetry carries with it a poignant sense of political burden. During her lifetime, she was held captive for a year because of her support of Protestant rebels, and created the edifice of what is known as the Church of England today. In the following poem, she examines the philosophical conundrum that busied philosophers during the middle ages: why do bad things happen to good people? Why do good things happen to bad people?

Written on a Wall at Woodstock

Oh Fortune, thy wresting wavering state

Hath fraught with cares my troubled wit,
Whose witness this present prison late
Could bear, where once was joy's loan quit.
Thou causedst the guilty to be loosed
From bands where innocents were inclosed,
And caused the guiltless to be reserved,
And freed those that death had well deserved.
But all herein can be nothing wrought,
So God send to my foes all they have thought.

ANNA LAETITIA BARBAULD
1743-1825

Educated at home by her mother, Anna Letitia Barbauld was influenced by the powerful female voices of the French Revolution, specifically Mary Wollestonecraft's *A Vindication of the Rights of Woman*. In the following ballad, Barbauld intends to push the buttons of fellow female listeners and readers. Though it vigorously begins as a call upon all women to use their knowledge and skills to fight for equal rights and even control their husbands, it ends somewhere radically different, away from dispute and hatred, in a manner that some may call peaceful.

The Rights of Woman

Yes, injured Woman! rise, assert thy right!
Woman! too long degraded, scorned, opprest;
O born to rule in partial Law's despite,
Resume thy native empire o'er the breast!

Go forth arrayed in panoply divine;
That angel pureness which admits no stain;
Go, bid proud Man his boasted rule resign,
And kiss the golden sceptre of thy reign.

Go, gird thyself with grace; collect thy store
Of bright artillery glancing from afar;
Soft melting tones thy thundering cannon's roar,
Blushes and fears thy magazine of war.

Thy rights are empire: urge no meaner claim,—
Felt, not defined, and if debated, lost;
Like sacred mysteries, which withheld from fame,
Shunning discussion, are revered the most.

Try all that wit and art suggest to bend
Of thy imperial foe the stubborn knee;
Make treacherous Man thy subject, not thy friend;
Thou mayst command, but never canst be free.

Awe the licentious, and restrain the rude;
Soften the sullen, clear the cloudy brow:
Be, more than princes' gifts, thy favours sued;—
She hazards all, who will the least allow.

But hope not, courted idol of mankind,
On this proud eminence secure to stay;
Subduing and subdued, thou soon shalt find
Thy coldness soften, and thy pride give way.

Then, then, abandon each ambitious thought,
Conquest or rule thy heart shall feebly move,
In Nature's school, by her soft maxims taught,
That separate rights are lost in mutual love.

PHILLIS WHEATLEY
1753-1784

Taught how to read and write by her masters, Wheatley is the first African-American female to publish widely and popularly throughout the States. Her poems are politically charged, often evoking the memory of George Washington, the Stamp Act, or the rebellious nature of American colonists. In the following poem, Wheatley accounts the rising tensions between the colonies and England by highlighting the soul's innate desire for freedom.

To The Right Honourable William, Earl Of Dartmouth, His Majesty's Principal Secretary Of The State For North-America

Hail, happy day, when, smiling like the morn,
Fair Freedom rose New-England to adorn:
The northern clime beneath her genial ray,
Dartmouth, congratulates thy blissful sway:
Elate with hope her race no longer mourns,
Each soul expands, each grateful bosom burns,
While in thine hand with pleasure we behold
The silken reins, and Freedom's charms unfold.
Long lost to realms beneath the northern skies
She shines supreme, while hated faction dies:
Soon as appear'd the Goddess long desir'd,

Sick at the view, she languish'd and expir'd;
Thus from the splendors of the morning light
The owl in sadness seeks the caves of night.
No more, America, in mournful strain
Of wrongs, and grievance unredress'd complain,
No longer shalt thou dread the iron chain,
Which wanton Tyranny with lawless hand
Had made, and with it meant t' enslave the land.
Should you, my lord, while you peruse my song,
Wonder from whence my love of Freedom sprung,
Whence flow these wishes for the common good,
By feeling hearts alone best understood,
I, young in life, by seeming cruel fate
Was snatch'd from Afric's fancy'd happy seat:
What pangs excruciating must molest,
What sorrows labour in my parent's breast?
Steel'd was that soul and by no misery mov'd
That from a father seiz'd his babe belov'd:
Such, such my case. And can I then but pray
Others may never feel tyrannic sway?
For favours past, great Sir, our thanks are due,
And thee we ask thy favours to renew,
Since in thy pow'r, as in thy will before,
To sooth the griefs, which thou did'st once deplore.
May heav'nly grace the sacred sanction give
To all thy works, and thou for ever live
Not only on the wings of fleeting Fame,
Though praise immortal crowns the patriot's name,
But to conduct to heav'ns refulgent fane,
May fiery coursers sweep th' ethereal plain,
And bear thee upwards to that blest abode,
Where, like the prophet, thou shalt find thy God.

AMY LOWELL
1874-1925

Amy Lowell disliked school, and found herself riddled with a lack of confidence because of what she considered overtly masculine and hideous features. Though her family lineage claimed a Harvard president and an astronomer, they did not believe it proper for a woman to go to college, so Lowell self-educated herself by reading anything she could get her eyes on. She was posthumously honored with a Nobel Peace Prize in 1926. The following poem juxtaposes America and Venice to represent the birth of a new world. Historically concise, the poem is also lyrically impressive as it uses the natural world as a symbol for the inner workings of government and politics.

1777

I
The Trumpet-Vine Arbour

The throats of the little red trumpet-flowers are wide open,
And the clangour of brass beats against the hot sunlight.
They bray and blare at the burning sky.

Red! Red! Coarse notes of red,
Trumpeted at the blue sky.
In long streaks of sound, molten metal,
The vine declares itself.
Clang! -- from its red and yellow trumpets.
Clang! -- from its long, nasal trumpets,
Splitting the sunlight into ribbons, tattered and shot with noise.
I sit in the cool arbour, in a green-and-gold twilight.
It is very still, for I cannot hear the trumpets,
I only know that they are red and open,
And that the sun above the arbour shakes with heat.
My quill is newly mended,
And makes fine-drawn lines with its point.
Down the long, white paper it makes little lines,
Just lines -- up -- down -- criss-cross.
My heart is strained out at the pin-point of my quill;
It is thin and writhing like the marks of the pen.
My hand marches to a squeaky tune,
It marches down the paper to a squealing of fifes.
My pen and the trumpet-flowers,
And Washington's armies away over the smoke-tree to the Southwest.
'Yankee Doodle,' my Darling! It is you against the British,
Marching in your ragged shoes to batter down King George.
What have you got in your hat? Not a feather, I wager.
Just a hay-straw, for it is the harvest you are fighting for.
Hay in your hat, and the whites of their eyes for a target!
Like Bunker Hill, two years ago, when I watched all day from the house-top
Through Father's spy-glass.
The red city, and the blue, bright water,
And puffs of smoke which you made.
Twenty miles away,

Round by Cambridge, or over the Neck,
But the smoke was white -- white!
To-day the trumpet-flowers are red -- red --
And I cannot see you fighting,
But old Mr. Dimond has fled to Canada,
And Myra sings 'Yankee Doodle' at her milking.
The red throats of the trumpets bray and clang in the sunshine,
And the smoke-tree puffs dun blossoms into the blue air.

II
The City of Falling Leaves
Leaves fall,
Brown leaves,
Yellow leaves streaked with brown.
They fall,
Flutter,
Fall again.
The brown leaves,
And the streaked yellow leaves,
Loosen on their branches
And drift slowly downwards.
One,
One, two, three,
One, two, five.
All Venice is a falling of Autumn leaves --
Brown,
And yellow streaked with brown.
'That sonnet, Abate,
Beautiful,
I am quite exhausted by it.
Your phrases turn about my heart
And stifle me to swooning.
Open the window, I beg.

Lord! What a strumming of fiddles and mandolins!
'Tis really a shame to stop indoors.
Call my maid, or I will make you lace me yourself.
Fie, how hot it is, not a breath of air!
See how straight the leaves are falling.
Marianna, I will have the yellow satin caught up with silver fringe,
It peeps out delightfully from under a mantle.
Am I well painted to-day, `caro Abate mio'?
You will be proud of me at the `Ridotto', hey?
Proud of being `Cavalier Servente' to such a lady?'
'Can you doubt it, `Bellissima Contessa'?
A pinch more rouge on the right cheek,
And Venus herself shines less . . .'
'You bore me, Abate,
I vow I must change you!
A letter, Achmet?
Run and look out of the window, Abate.
I will read my letter in peace.'
The little black slave with the yellow satin turban
Gazes at his mistress with strained eyes.
His yellow turban and black skin
Are gorgeous -- barbaric.
The yellow satin dress with its silver flashings
Lies on a chair
Beside a black mantle and a black mask.
Yellow and black,
Gorgeous -- barbaric.
The lady reads her letter,
And the leaves drift slowly
Past the long windows.
'How silly you look, my dear Abate,
With that great brown leaf in your wig.
Pluck it off, I beg you,

Or I shall die of laughing.'
A yellow wall
Aflare in the sunlight,
Chequered with shadows,
Shadows of vine leaves,
Shadows of masks.
Masks coming, printing themselves for an instant,
Then passing on,
More masks always replacing them.
Masks with tricorns and rapiers sticking out behind
Pursuing masks with plumes and high heels,
The sunlight shining under their insteps.
One,
One, two,
One, two, three,
There is a thronging of shadows on the hot wall,
Filigreed at the top with moving leaves.
Yellow sunlight and black shadows.
Yellow and black,
Gorgeous -- barbaric.
Two masks stand together,
And the shadow of a leaf falls through them,
Marking the wall where they are not.
From hat-tip to shoulder-tip,
From elbow to sword-hilt,
The leaf falls.
The shadows mingle,
Blur together,
Slide along the wall and disappear.
Gold of mosaics and candles,
And night blackness lurking in the ceiling beams.
Saint Mark's glitters with flames and reflections.
A cloak brushes aside,
And the yellow of satin

Licks out over the coloured inlays of the pavement.
Under the gold crucifixes
There is a meeting of hands
Reaching from black mantles.
Sighing embraces, bold investigations,
Hide in confessionals,
Sheltered by the shuffling of feet.
Gorgeous – barbaric
In its mail of jewels and gold,
Saint Mark's looks down at the swarm of black masks;
And outside in the palace gardens brown leaves fall,
Flutter,
Fall.
Brown,
And yellow streaked with brown.
Blue-black, the sky over Venice,
With a pricking of yellow stars.
There is no moon,
And the waves push darkly against the prow
Of the gondola,
Coming from Malamocco
And streaming toward Venice.
It is black under the gondola hood,
But the yellow of a satin dress
Glares out like the eye of a watching tiger.
Yellow compassed about with darkness,
Yellow and black,
Gorgeous -- barbaric.
The boatman sings,
It is Tasso that he sings;
The lovers seek each other beneath their mantles,
And the gondola drifts over the lagoon, aslant to the coming dawn.
But at Malamocco in front,

In Venice behind,
Fall the leaves,
Brown,
And yellow streaked with brown.
They fall,
Flutter,
Fall.

ISABELLA WHITNEY
1548-1573

In her short life, Isabella Whitney left a legacy that recognizes her as the first English woman to publish secularized poetry. Interesting to note, scholars, for the most part, have abandoned Whitney; her name was not even listed in the encyclopedia-anthology edited by C.S. Lewis, *British Literature in the Sixteenth Century* (1954). I suppose this should not come as a surprise: though animated, soulful, and intelligent her writing may be, she was still a woman. In the following poem, imagining life existing without her in it, Whitney pays homage to the particularities of London: the bookkeepers, the street-lights, and the people who no one else notices except for her during her nightly walks.

from The Manner of Her Will, & What She Left to London, and to All Those in It, at Her Departing

I whole in body, and in mind,
    but very weak in purse,
Do make, and write my testament
    for fear it will be worse.
And first I wholly do commend

my soul and body eke,
To God the Father and the Son,
    so long as I can speak.
And after speech, my soul to him,
    and body to the grave,
Till time that all shall rise again,
    their Judgement for to have,
And then I hope they both shall meet,
    to dwell for aye in joy;
Whereas I trust to see my friends
    released from all annoy.
Thus have you heard touching my soul,
    and body what I mean:
I trust you all will witness bear,
    I have a steadfast brain.
O God, now let me dispose such things,
    as I shall leave behind,
That those which shall receive the same,
    may know my willing mind.
I first of all to London leave,
    because I there was bred,
Brave buildings rare, of churches store,
    and Paul's to the head.
Between the same, fair treats there be,
    and people goodly store;
Because their keeping craveth cost,
    I yet will leave him more.
First for their food, I butchers leave,
    that every day shall kill;
By Thames you shall have brewers' store,
    and bakers at your will.
And such as orders do observe,
    and eat fish thrice a week,
I leave two streets, full fraught therewith,

they need not far to seek.
Watling Street, and Canwick Street,
    I full of woolen leave;
And linen store in Friday Street,
    if they me not deceive.
And those which are of calling such,
    that costlier they require,
I mercers leave, with silk so rich,
    as any would desire.
In Cheap of them, they store shall find,
    and likewise in that street,
I goldsmiths leave, with jewels such,
    as are for ladies meet.

      * * *

Now when the folk are fed and clad
    with such as I have named,
For dainty mouths, and stomachs weak
    some junckets must be framed.
Wherefore I potecaries leave,
    with banquets in their shop,
Physicians also for the sick,
    Diseases for to stop.
Some roysters still must bide in thee,
    and such as cut it out;
That with the guiltless quarrel will,
    to let their blood about.
For them I cunning surgeons leave,
    some plasters to apply,
That ruffians may not still be hanged,
    nor quiet persons die.

      * * *

To all the bookbinders by Paul's,
    because I like their art,
They every week shall money have,
    when they from books depart.
Among them all, my printer must
    have somewhat to his share;
I will my friends these books to buy
    of him, with other ware.
For maidens poor, I widowers rich
    do leave, that oft shall dote:
And by that means shall marry them,
    to set the girls afloat.
And wealthy widows will I leave
    to help young gentlemen;
Which when you have, in any case,
    be courteous to them then:
And see their plate and jewels eke
    may not be marred with rust;
Nor let their bags too long be full,
    for fear that they do burst.

        * * *

And Bedlam must not be forgot,
    for that was oft my walk:
I people there too many leave,
    that out of tune do talk.

        * * *

At th' Inns of Court, I lawyers leave
    to take their case in hand.
And also leave I at each Inn

    of Court, or Chancery,
Of gentlemen, a youthful roote,
    full of activity,
For whom I store of books have left,
    at each bookbinder's stall:
And part of all that London hath,
    to furnish them withal.
And when they are with study cloyed,
    to recreate their mind,
Of tennis courts, of dancing schools,
    and fence they store shall find.
And every Sunday at the least,
    I leave to make them sport,
In divers places players, that
    of wonders shall report.
Now, London, have I (for thy sake)
    within thee, and without,
As comes into my memory,
    dispersèd 'round about
Such needful things as they should have,
    here left now unto thee;
When I am gone, with conscience,
    let them dispersèd be.
And though I nothing namèd have,
    to bury me withal,
Consider that above the ground,
    annoyance be I shall.
And let me have a shrouding sheet
    to cover me from shame,
And in oblivion bury me,
    and never more me name.
Ringings nor other ceremonies
    use you not for cost,
Nor at my burial, make no feast,

your money were but lost.

* * *

This XX of October, I,
    in ANNO DOMINI,
A thousand, v. hundred seventy-three,
    as almanacs descry,
Did write this will with mine own hand,
    and it to London gave;
In witness of the standers-by,
    whose names, if you will have,
paper, pen and standish were,
    at that same present by,
With Time, who promised to reveal
    so fast as she could buy
The same, lest of my nearer kin
    for any thing should vary;
So finally I make an end
    no longer can I tarry.

EMMA LAZARUS
1849-1887

Daughter of Moses and Esther Lazarus, Emma Lazarus's family were Sephardic Jews who emigrated from Portugal to New York during the Colonial era. She writes often about her Jewish ancestry and its relationship to the Americas and her faith, but is most famous for her poem "The New Colossus" which is etched permanently in gold on a plaque at the Statue of Liberty. Offering insight into the somewhat understudied scholarship of early Jewish American history, the following sonnet celebrates the New World's acceptance of a people who the "West refused and the East abhorred." Today, especially, it serves as a reminder of the welcoming and open spirit deeply rooted in American culture.

1492

Thou two-faced year, Mother of Change and Fate,
Didst weep when Spain cast forth with flaming sword,
The children of the prophets of the Lord,
Prince, priest, and people, spurned by zealot hate.
Hounded from sea to sea, from state to state,
The West refused them, and the East abhorred.

No anchorage the known world could afford,
Close-locked was every port, barred every gate.
Then smiling, thou unveil'dst, O two-faced year,
A virgin world where doors of sunset part,
Saying, "Ho, all who weary, enter here!
There falls each ancient barrier that the art
Of race or creed or rank devised, to rear
Grim bulwarked hatred between heart and heart!"

THE IN BETWEEN

I heard a Fly buzz – when I died –
The Stillness in the Room
-Emily Dickinson

Contemporary readers may automatically think of Sylvia Plath as a poet of the in between. Plath, who took her life, managed to become a master poet by the age of thirty. Indeed, the voices in this section express the haunting primeval anxieties that came before her, that perhaps spoke to her, as I hope they will speak to you. We begin our journey into the inner-gyre of our consciousness with none other than Emily Brontë, whose first and only novel *Wuthering Heights* still finds international fame because of its addictingly cryptic dark narrative.

To describe what the following poems capture, what they intend to convey, the ethereal shutter of the unconscious, the lost moments of the mind outside of the self, the chaotic array of individuality, well to describe all of this would take a poem. Many of these voices turn to dreamlands in an attempt to escape the containment of everyday life; others simply break the boundaries of what would have been considered accepted womanly thoughts. The following poems bring the ineffable stuff of the in between into a tangible, existing reality.

EMILY BRONTË
1818-1848

The daughter of Patrick Brontë and Maria Branwell, the Brontë sister claims a lineage of literary excellence. Emily Brontë's *Wuthering Heights*, with its stunning articulation of violence and passion urged many readers to believe it was written by the hands of a man. In the following poem, the use of the refrain "I cannot go" embodies the mysterious seduction of a dark night. In repeating her will not to go, the speaker accepts the truth that she has, without will, yielded to "the tyrant spell."

Spellbound

The night is darkening round me,
The wild winds coldly blow;
But a tyrant spell has bound me
And I cannot, cannot go.

The giant trees are bending
Their bare boughs weighed with snow.
And the storm is fast descending,
And yet I cannot go.

Clouds beyond clouds above me,

Wastes beyond wastes below;
But nothing drear can move me;
I will not, cannot go.

CHRISTINA ROSSETTI
1830-1894

Some poets believe that lucid dreaming is the finest state of connecting with the inner-self. In the following poem, Christina Rossetti offers readers insight into the sojourn of a newly departed soul from one land (the physical) to another (the ineffable). The poet utilizes the art of rhyme to comfort readers with its lulling musicality. Every third line interrupts the rhyme, as might a bob in medieval poetry, to perhaps signify the shock and otherness of this new world.

Dream Land

Where sunless rivers weep
Their waves into the deep,
She sleeps a charmed sleep:
    Awake her not.
Led by a single star,
She came from very far
To seek where shadows are
    Her pleasant lot.

She left the rosy morn,
She left the fields of corn,
For twilight cold and lorn
    And water springs.

Through sleep, as through a veil,
She sees the sky look pale,
And hears the nightingale
    That sadly sings.

Rest, rest, a perfect rest
Shed over brow and breast;
Her face is toward the west,
    The purple land.
She cannot see the grain
Ripening on hill and plain;
She cannot feel the rain
    Upon her hand.

Rest, rest, for evermore
Upon a mossy shore;
Rest, rest at the heart's core
    Till time shall cease:
Sleep that no pain shall wake;
Night that no morn shall break
Till joy shall overtake
    Her perfect peace.

MARY DARBY ROBINSON
1758-1800

Perhaps it is comforting for you to know that one day, probably more than once, Mary Darby Robinson opened her eyes without the slightest desire to move her body from her bed. The sunlight burned. The birds' song clawed at her ears. Her legs urged *stay*. We've all had those days. The following sonnet intensifies the mounting pressures the speaker feels to keep up her happiness. The poet is able to aptly express the mounting constrains of her day to day life by keeping to the tightly woven fourteen line structure and rhyme scheme of the form.

Sonnet XXI: Why Do I Live

Why do I live to loath the cheerful day,
To shun the smiles of Fame, and mark the hours
On tardy pinions move, while ceaseless show'rs
Down my wan cheek in lucid currents stray?
My tresses all abound, nor gems display,
Nor scents Arabian! on my path no flow'rs
Imbibe the morn's resuscitating pow'rs,
For one blank sorrow, saddens all my way!
As slow the radiant Sun of reason rose,
Through tears my dying parents saw it shine;

A brother's frailties, swell'd the tide of woes,-
And, keener far, maternal griefs were mine!
Phaon! if soon these weary eyes shall close,
Oh! must that task, that mournful task, be thine?

SARA TEASDALE
1884-1933

Born in Chicago into a devout and established family, Sara Teasdale had such poor health as a child that she could not attend school until she was fourteen years of age. She took her own life via an overdose on sleeping pills after publishing six collections of poetry; her book *A Strange Victory* was published posthumously. The following poem, which was included in her first published collection, can be interpreted in many different ways. In understanding Teasdale's suicide, depression, and addiction, some may understand it as a representation of the harm of those things that numb the mind of pain, and later, after use after use after use, numb the soul of emotional validation and physical consciousness.

House of Dreams

You took my empty dreams
And filled them every one
With tenderness and nobleness,
April and the sun.

The old empty dreams
Where my thoughts would throng
Are far too full of happiness
To even hold a song.

Oh, the empty dreams were dim
And the empty dreams were wide,
They were sweet and shadowy houses
Where my thoughts could hide.

But you took my dreams away
And you made them all come true --
My thoughts have no place now to play,
And nothing now to do.

JANE AUSTEN
1775-1817

Connected by the electricity of their creative intelligence, Austen shared friendships with Albert Einstein and Charles Darwin throughout her lifetime. Her intellectual capabilities were unmatched; she was knowledgeable on aspects of Mathematics, Law, and the Soul. The following poem evokes Ovid's retelling of Philomela, who, after being raped and slain by her brother-in-law, transformed into a nightingale.

Ode to Pity

1

Ever musing I delight to tread
The Paths of honour and the Myrtle Grove
Whilst the pale Moon her beams doth shed
On disappointed Love.
While Philomel on airy hawthorn Bush
Sings sweet and Melancholy, And the thrush
Converses with the Dove.

2

Gently brawling down the turnpike road,
Sweetly noisy falls the Silent Stream--
The Moon emerges from behind a Cloud

And darts upon the Myrtle Grove her beam.
Ah! then what Lovely Scenes appear,
The hut, the Cot, the Grot, and Chapel queer,
And eke the Abbey too a mouldering heap,
Cnceal'd by aged pines her head doth rear
And quite invisible doth take a peep.

EMILY DICKINSON
1830-1886

What would contemporary poetry be without Emily Dickinson? Her religious and sexual ambiguity and fascination with death attracts the youngest to the oldest of readers. Her delicate use of rhyme undercuts the severity of her content, as is seen in the following poem, which praises the ethereal realm of dreamscapes. The majority of Dickinson's poems were published posthumously; today there are endless prestigious poetry awards named in her honor.

We Dream -- it is Good we are Dreaming

We dream -- it is good we are dreaming --
It would hurt us -- were we awake --
But since it is playing -- kill us,
And we are playing -- shriek --

What harm? Men die -- externally --
It is a truth -- of Blood --
But we -- are dying in Drama --
And Drama -- is never dead --

Cautious -- We jar each other --

And either -- open the eyes --
Lest the Phantasm -- prove the Mistake --
And the livid Surprise

Cool us to Shafts of Granite --
With just an Age -- and Name --
And perhaps a phrase in Egyptian --
It's prudenter -- to dream --

AMY LOWELL
1874-1925

Ciphering through Lowell's complex soundscapes may give first-time readers some difficulty. I urge you, swallow her words. Read them aloud. Rather than romanticizing the natural world, the following poem meditates on the brutality of the act of picking flowers with their heinous scents. The poem's title says it all: it is a morose perspective of the beautiful.

Grotesque

Why do the lilies goggle their tongues at me
When I pluck them;
And writhe and twist,
And strangle themselves against my fingers,
So that I can hardly weave the garland
For your hair?
Why do they shriek your name
And spit at me
When I would cluster them?
Must I kill them
To make them lie still,
And send you a wreath of lolling corpses
To turn putrid and soft
On your forehead
While you dance?

ANNE KINGSMILL FINCH
1661-1720

Finch was deeply inspired by the movements of the Restoration, the Cavaliers, and the metaphysical poets. She was an aristocratic poet, and lived a life that afforded her the luxury of time to create; yet she was burdened with an acute awareness of the injustices in her world. In the following poem the speaker bolding proclaims that it is her "bus'ness...to dye", expresses her will to directly surrender to the influence of departure.

To Death

O King of Terrors, whose unbounded Sway
All that have Life, must certainly Obey;
The King, the Priest, the Prophet, all are Thine,
Nor wou'd ev'n God (in Flesh) thy Stroke decline.
My Name is on thy Roll, and sure I must
Encrease thy gloomy Kingdom in the Dust.
My soul at this no Apprehension feels,
But trembles at thy Swords, thy Racks, thy Wheels;
Thy scorching Fevers, which distract the Sense,
And snatch us raving, unprepar'd from hence;
At thy contagious Darts, that wound the Heads
Of weeping Friends, who wait at dying Beds.
Spare these, and let thy Time be when it will;

My Bus'ness is to Dye, and Thine to Kill.
Gently thy fatal Sceptre on me lay,
And take to thy cold Arms, insensibly, thy Prey.

MOTHER - NATURE - RAIN

To What Purpose, April, do you return again?
Beauty is not enough.
-Edna St. Vincent Millay

In order to describe their inner turmoil, the Romantics turned to the outside world, more specifically the weather. The thundering clouds above somehow expressed the clamoring of emotions within the character. The Japanese have long had an affinity with the natural world, praising its enigmatic grandeur in their poetry. Nationwide, college curriculums have created courses in Eco-poetics, a study of poetry entirely devoted to the psychology and influence of nature.

All at once we live in unity and at odds with the natural world. We want to control it, we desire to understand it, to know what it will do -- what will the weekend forecast bring? How bad will the snowstorm be? -- While at the same time we are in awe of its infinite and ineffable beauty. In a way, nature has an unconscious control over us: when the wind is wild and the sky is gray we feel compelled to stay inside; when the sun shines and the flowers bloom we excuse ourselves from within the walls and bask in the glory of the outside world. It is impossible to avoid nature. The following poems meditate on such, dare I say natural, wonders.

LI QUINGZHAU CI
1081-1141

Born into a family of government officials and scholars, Li Quingzhau's father was a student of popular Chinese poet and painter Su Shi. Young Li Quingzhau Ci had an effervescent personality: she was outgoing, thoughtful, and expressive. While there are assumed to be only around one hundred of her poems known to survive, she is considered a prominent poet of the Song Dynasty, with scholars often commending the elegant restraint in her verse. The following poem delicately traces the ending of one season and the beginning of the next.

Huan Xi Sha

The small courtyard through my deep
window: Out there Spring grows old.
When I unroll the blinds they cast

evening shadows so that I am at a loss
for words. Clouds gather, haze sits
on the mountains, the light

rain reminds us of dusk.

HELEN GRAY CONE
1859-1936

In New York City, Helen Gray Cone is celebrated for her legacy at Hunter College, where she was educated and later solidified her career. Cone dedicated her life to teaching, reading, and writing; today, an honorarium is still given in her name at her alma mater. The following sonnet examines the memory of a summer-walk. Cone's elegant weaving of sounds enliven the image of a world ready for rebirth.

In Winter, With The Book We Read In Spring

The blackberry's bloom, when last we went this way,
Veiled all her bowsome rods with trembling white;
The robin's sunset breast gave forth delight
At sunset hour; the wind was warm with May.
Armored in ice the sere stems arch to-day,
Each tiny thorn encased and argent bright;
Where clung the birds that long have taken flight,
Dead songless leaves cling fluttering on the spray.

O hand in mine, that mak'st all paths the same,
Being paths of peace, where falls nor chill nor gloom,
Made sweet with ardors of an inward spring!
I hold thee-frozen skies to rosy flame
Are turned, and snows to living snows of bloom,
And once again the gold-brown thrushes sing.

H.D. (Hilda Doolittle)
1886-1961

When H.D. pulls away from her work, she reveals. When she focuses in, she enlivens and complicates the simple. Her work is almost impossible to pin down. She witnessed the political divide of the bourgeois and the proletariat, the industrial revolution, and the two great World wars. These shifting convictions of the globe survive through her poetry. The following poem exists in two dimensions; the first attempts a modernized control over nature, while the second begs for the natural world to save the speaker - it is hot, and she wants a breeze. "Garden" is an intelligent, provocative, and complicated manipulation of the unknown.

Garden

I
You are clear
O rose, cut in rock,
hard as the descent of hail.

I could scrape the colour
from the petals
like spilt dye from a rock.

If I could break you
I could break a tree.

If I could stir
I could break a tree—
I could break you.

II
O wind, rend open the heat,
cut apart the heat,
rend it to tatters.

Fruit cannot drop
through this thick air—
fruit cannot fall into heat
that presses up and blunts
the points of pears
and rounds the grapes.

Cut the heat—
plough through it,
turning it on either side
of your path.

EMILY DICKINSON
1830-1886

Dickinson lived her life unrecognized for her lyrical talent, a sentiment many emerging writers may empathize with. Imagine the Dickinson's writing out there today! She spent the later half of her life baking for her family, tending to her garden, and observing the inner-workings of society. Her command of form within her verse, as well as her control of philosophical wonderings, is still unparalleled. The following poem personifies nature as a female, enhancing her divine glory.

Nature, the Gentlest Mother

Nature, the gentlest mother,
Impatient of no child,
The feeblest or the waywardest, —
Her admonition mild

In forest and the hill
By traveller is heard,
Restraining rampant squirrel
Or too impetuous bird.

How fair her conversation,

A summer afternoon, —
Her household, her assembly;
And when the sun goes down

Her voice among the aisles
Incites the timid prayer
Of the minutest cricket,
The most unworthy flower.

When all the children sleep
She turns as long away
As will suffice to light her lamps;
Then, bending from the sky

With infinite affection
And infiniter care,
Her golden finger on her lip,
Wills silence everywhere.

ELLA WHEELER WILCOX
1850-1919

Born on a farm in Johnstown, Wisconsin, Ella Wheeler Wilcox began writing poetry at a young age, and built up a reputation as the poet of her town by the time she finished high school. The aesthetic lineation of the following poem mimics the changing of emotions of the speaker. In typical Romantic fashion, it connects nature and human sentimentality: how the weather appears in the poem is meant to represent how the speaker feels.

Bleak Weather

Dear love, where the red lillies blossomed and grew,
The white snows are falling;
And all through the wood, where I wandered with you,
The loud winds are calling;
And the robin that piped to us tune upon tune,
Neath the elm—you remember,
Over tree-top and mountain has followed the June,
And left us—December.

Has left, like a friend that is true in the sun,
And false in the shadows.
He has found new delights, in the land where he's gone,

Greener woodlands and meadows.
What care we? let him go! let the snow shroud the lea,
Let it drift on the heather!
We can sing through it all; I have you—you have me,
And we'll laugh at the weather.

The old year may die, and a new one be born
That is bleaker and colder;
But it cannot dismay us; we dare it—we scorn,
For love makes us bolder.
Ah Robin! sing loud on the far-distant lea,
Thou friend in fair weather;
But here is a song sung, that's fuller of glee,
By two warm hearts together.

ANNE KINGSMILL FINCH
1661-1720

Finch is said to have been able to write with a concise perspicuity of what she witnessed. If that's true, when she observed nature, what she must have seen was a kaleidoscope of color and shape, a world whose imaginative landscape spans farther than many of us could envision. The following homage to the tree -- an under appreciated vessel of life in contemporary culture (yet of the highest necessity) -- validates our emotional connection to nature.

The Tree

Fair tree! for thy delightful shade
'Tis just that some return be made;
Sure some return is due from me
To thy cool shadows, and to thee.
When thou to birds dost shelter give,
Thou music dost from them receive;
If travellers beneath thee stay
Till storms have worn themselves away,
That time in praising thee they spend
And thy protecting pow'r commend.
The shepherd here, from scorching freed,
Tunes to thy dancing leaves his reed;

Whilst his lov'd nymph, in thanks, bestows
Her flow'ry chaplets on thy boughs.
Shall I then only silent be,
And no return be made by me?
No; let this wish upon thee wait,
And still to flourish be thy fate.
To future ages may'st thou stand
Untouch'd by the rash workman's hand,
Till that large stock of sap is spent,
Which gives thy summer's ornament;
Till the fierce winds, that vainly strive
To shock thy greatness whilst alive,
Shall on thy lifeless hour attend,
Prevent the axe, and grace thy end;
Their scatter'd strength together call
And to the clouds proclaim thy fall;
Who then their ev'ning dews may spare
When thou no longer art their care,
But shalt, like ancient heroes, burn,
And some bright hearth be made thy urn.

EMILY BRONTË
1818-1848

While H.D. begged for the wind to come and save her from the sweltering heat, Brontë describes the calamitous power of the wind. In her novels, the wind is used to represent the powerful emotions of her characters. The following poem begins by utilizing the vibratory sound of the letter "H" to control the breath of readers. This silent and invisible breath also mimic the flow of the wind. The poem is a tumultuous whirlwind of language.

High waving heather, 'neath stormy blasts bending

High waving heather, 'neath stormy blasts bending,
Midnight and moonlight and bright shining stars;
Darkness and glory rejoicingly blending,
Earth rising to heaven and heaven descending,
Man's spirit away from its drear dongeon sending,
Bursting the fetters and breaking the bars.

All down the mountain sides, wild forest lending
One mighty voice to the life-giving wind;
Rivers their banks in the jubilee rending,
Fast through the valleys a reckless course wending,
Wider and deeper their waters extending,

Leaving a desolate desert behind.
Shining and lowering and swelling and dying,
Changing for ever from midnight to noon;
Roaring like thunder, like soft music sighing,
Shadows on shadows advancing and flying,
Lightning-bright flashes the deep gloom defying,
Coming as swiftly and fading as soon.

LOVE SONGS

He's more myself than I am. Whatever our souls are made of, his and mine are the same.
-Wuthering Heights, **Emily Brontë**

Philosopher Erich Fromm begins the second chapter of his book *The Art of Loving* with the following quotation: "Love: The answer to the problem of human existence." In every language, in every culture, societies crave love. Familial, erotic, sensualized, or forbidden, love motivates the mind, it plays with the ego, it stirs the passions our consciousness until we feel sick; indeed, lovesickness was a common theme of many Medieval and sixteenth century courtly poetry.

Love is everlasting. It is undefinable. It is everything. The following poems elucidate the multifaceted landscapes of love.

MINA LOY
1882-1966

Admired by T.S. Elliot, Gertrude Stein, Ezra Pound, and other powerhouse poets of the Modernist era, Mina Loy is still a celebrated poet in modernist circles. Pound is said to have wondered, in a letter written to Marianne Moore, if "anyone in the world of poetry wrote as interestingly" as she and Mina Loy. Loy's poetry is piercing and provocative, and the tumultuous thundering of sounds highlights the dangerous nature of love in the following poem. It is the final image that seems the most accurate portrayal of what love might look like if it were ever in solid form.

Love Songs

Spawn of Fantasies
Silting the appraisable
Pig Cupid his rosy snout
Rooting erotic garbage
'Once upon a time'
Pulls a weed white star-topped
Among wild oats sown in mucous-membrane

I would an eye in a Bengal light
Eternity in a sky-rocket
Constellations in an ocean
Whose rivers run no fresher
Than a trickle of saliva

These are suspect places

I must live in my lantern
Trimming subliminal flicker
Virginal to the bellows
Of Experience

Coloured glass

ANNE BRADSTREET
1612-1672

Bradstreet's stunning ability to extend the metaphor of union in the following poem has sustained its voice through the years, helping it achieve wide popularity in contemporary and secularized wedding ceremonies across the world. Its message is simple and clear. Bradstreet's love is grateful, bountiful, and eternal. The following poem is a true love song.

To My Dear Loving Husband

If ever two were one, then surely we.
If ever man were loved by wife, then thee;
If ever wife was happy in a man,
Compare with me ye women if you can.
I prize thy love more than whole mines of gold,
Or all the riches that the East doth hold.
My love is such that rivers cannot quench,
Nor ought but love from thee give recompense.
Thy love is such I can no way repay;
The heavens reward thee manifold, I pray.
Then while we live, in love let's so persever
That when we live no more we may live ever.

SAPPHO
630/612-570 BC

Though traditional in its history as a love poem composed specifically for the bride on her walk to the wedding chamber, the epithalamion is still a popular form of poetry today. Here, Sappho puts her longing and desires aside to celebrate the unification of lovers. However, the poem is still genuinely erotic in its honoring of the couple's first night together, and, one assumes, their first copulation. For this translation, most of all, I have tried to keep the musicality of Sappho's poem in order preserve the celebratory tone of this joyous tradition.

Epithalamion

Sing the Evening Song!
See the moon gleam on the shore?
Break from dinner dear children
and play for us a ribald!
On this altar we will sing
of matrimonial bliss; the sun
has set dear children. The bride-
groom has been waiting for this.
Let's guide our merry watchers
across the fair groom's plain,

the sun has set dear children.
Burn bright her bridal flame!

Look, young man, look--
your faithful bride is here;
take her gently with your hands
to ease her footsteps' fears.

Sharp, young man, sharp,
stand straight as the mighty oak.
Branch out fruitfully as the vine
and your bride will cling at your coat.
...
Do I yearn for yesteryear
those morrows on the mountain cliff
watching closely the drop of land
and the rising of the mist
of Aegean's blue unknown?
Could it be I wish, nay, I miss,
first melting into Cercolas, that
last breath with virgin lips?

EMMA LAZARUS
1849-1887

The sculpture off which Emma Lazarus's poem is based off of was created around 100-130 B.C., dating the roots of this poem over one thousand years prior to the poet's own lifetime. Honoring the Greek goddess of love and beauty, Aphrodite, Lazarus brings to life the inanimate object. In the following poem, Lazarus juxtaposes the act of bearing witness to the statue for the first time with the act of encountering a first love.

Venus of the Louvre

Down the long hall she glistens like a star,
The foam-born mother of Love, transfixed to stone,
Yet none the less immortal, breathing on.
Time's brutal hand hath maimed but could not mar.
When first the enthralled enchantress from afar
Dazzled mine eyes, I saw not her alone,
Serenely poised on her world-worshipped throne,
As when she guided once her dove-drawn car,—
But at her feet a pale, death-stricken Jew,
Her life adorer, sobbed farewell to love.
Here Heine wept! Here still he weeps anew,
Nor ever shall his shadow lift or move,

While mourns one ardent heart, one poet-brain,
For vanished Hellas and Hebraic pain.

KATHERINE PHILLIPS
1632-1664

As a member of the Society of Friendship, a religious movement of the Quakers, Phillips preached the importance of Platonic Love: much of her writing expresses the virtues of the ideal woman who is chaste, proper, and filled with virtue. The following poem defies such expectations as the speaker confronts her inability to cherish the sanctity of love. It is an accurate portrayal of the pains of love.

Against Love

Hence Cupid! with your cheating toys,
Your real griefs, and painted joys,
Your pleasure which itself destroys.
Lovers like men in fevers burn and rave,
And only what will injure them do crave.
Men's weakness makes love so severe,
They give him power by their fear,
And make the shackles which they wear.
Who to another does his heart submit,
Makes his own idol, and then worships it.
Him whose heart is all his own,
Peace and liberty does crown,
He apprehends no killing frown.
He feels no raptures which are joys diseased,
And is not much transported, but still pleased.

MARY DARBY ROBINSON
1758-1800

Mary Darby Robinson is quoted to have said, "Every event of my life has more or less been marked by the progressive evils of a too acute sensibility. " In the following poem, this acute awareness of love is profoundly dissected. The poem questions love's power, it honors loves divinity, and it wonders if this emotional concept known to bring down great men and countries could ever compare to the grandeur of the natural world.

Stanzas to Love

Tell me, love, when I rove o'er some far distant plain,
Shall I cherish the passion that dwells in my breast?
Or will absence subdue the keen rigours of pain,
And the swift wing of time bring the balsam of rest?
Shall the image of him I was born to adore,
Inshrin'd in my bosom my idol still prove?
Or seduced by caprice shall fine feeling no more,
With the incense of truth gem the altar of love?
When I view the deep tint of the dew-dropping Rose,
Where the bee sits enamour'd its nectar to sip;
Then, ah say, will not memory fondly disclose
The softer vermilion that glow'd on his lip?
Will the sun when he rolls in his chariot of fire,

So dazzle my mind with the glare of his rays,
That my senses one moment shall cease to admire
The more perfect refulgence that beam'd in his lays?
When the shadows of twilight steal over the plain,
And the nightingale pours its lorn plaint in the grove,
Ah! will not the fondness that thrills thro' the strain,
Then recall to my mind his dear accents of Love!
When I gaze on the stars that bespangle the sky,
Ah! will not their mildness some pity inspire;
Like the soul-touching softness that beam'd in his eye,
When the tear of regret chill'd the flame of desire?
Then spare, thou dear Urchin, thou soother of pain,
Oh! spare the sweet picture engrav'd on my heart;
As a record of love let it ever remain;
My bosom thy tablet thy pencil a dart.

MOREOVER, THE MOON

***The first time that the sun rose on thine oath
to love me, I looked forward to the moon
-Elizabeth Barrett Browning***

Luminous. Multifaceted. Ever-changing and dominating; sometimes full, sometimes sleek. The eternalized symbol of the female principle, the moon's ineffable control on human existence is undeniable. Middle age legend believes that the Moon was full when Sodom and Gomorrah were destroyed, adding to its mysterious malevolent power. Her beautiful brilliance captivates onlookers. She controls the tide, the liquidy substance of earth. In French astrology, lunar facial features alluded to innocence or naiveté. The moon is believed to control the brain; consider the etymology of the word lunacy, from the latin "luna." Today, astrologers and meteorologists alike understand that the position of the moon is as important as the position of the sun.

She is bold. She is brilliant. She is other-worldly. There is no other thing in our universe connected to the female spirit quite like the moon.

MINA LOY
1882-1966

The daughter of Sigmund Lowry and Julian Byran, Mina Loy studied painting, theatre, and writing as a child. She maintained her posture as a critical figure in the avante-garde movement in Paris and in New York. Loy's direct, confessional style shocked readers of the time, and her bravery is only equalled to her fierce linguistic originality. In the following poem, Loy endures the difficult undertaking of articulating the ineffable power of the moon.

Moreover the Moon –

Face of the skies
preside
over our wonder.

Fluorescent
truant of heaven
draw us under.

Silver, circular corpse
your decease
infects us with unendurable ease,

touching nerve-terminals
to thermal icicles

Coercive as coma, frail as bloom
innuendoes of your inverse dawn
suffuse the self;
our every corpuscle become an elf.

SAPPHO
630/612-570 BC

Comparing her heartache to the blindness from a brightly lit night sky that prevents the watcher from seeing the miracle of the stars, Sappho reconstructs the notion of a romantic, moonlit evening. In the following poem, the speaker, forlorn, addresses the side effect of love-sickness that strips its victim from happiness. She borrows the feminine luster of the moon to highlight the magnitude of her love.

Moon and Stars

As the moon lights fully the sills of heaven
so her beams form beacons brightening the earth
from the silvery shining clusters of stars,
shielding their faces,
so does Anactoria's beauty blind me
so that my sight grows dim and even the joy
Gorgo, Atthis, and Gyrinno give me fades
dark from my vision.

ELIZABETH BARRETT BROWNING
1806-1861

Invoked by the eerie tone of first two lines in which the day "perished silently", the nocturnal qualities of Elizabeth Barrett Browning's "A Sea-side Walk" send haunting chills down the reader's back. In the poem, the sky is empty, and the weird temperament of the absence of the moon adds to the ominous aura of the poem. In the following poem, a nightly walk beside the sea leads to an important inner discovery.

A Sea-side Walk

We walked beside the sea,
After a day which perished silently
Of its own glory---like the Princess weird
Who, combating the Genius, scorched and seared,
Uttered with burning breath, 'Ho! victory!'
And sank adown, an heap of ashes pale;
So runs the Arab tale.

The sky above us showed
An universal and unmoving cloud,
On which, the cliffs permitted us to see
Only the outline of their majesty,

As master-minds, when gazed at by the crowd!
And, shining with a gloom, the water grey
Swang in its moon-taught way.

Nor moon nor stars were out.
They did not dare to tread so soon about,
Though trembling, in the footsteps of the sun.
The light was neither night's nor day's, but one
Which, life-like, had a beauty in its doubt;
And Silence's impassioned breathings round
Seemed wandering into sound.

O solemn-beating heart
Of nature! I have knowledge that thou art
Bound unto man's by cords he cannot sever---
And, what time they are slackened by him ever,
So to attest his own supernal part,
Still runneth thy vibration fast and strong,
The slackened cord along.

For though we never spoke
Of the grey water anal the shaded rock,---
Dark wave and stone, unconsciously, were fused
Into the plaintive speaking that we used,
Of absent friends and memories unforsook;
And, had we seen each other's face, we had
Seen haply, each was sad.

MARY DARBY ROBINSON
1758-1800

Born to the naval captain John Darby, Mary Darby Robinson was a celebrated figure in England: she was an actress, a playwright, a poet, a novelist, and the first publicized Mistress of the Prince of Wales, later to be known as King George IV. Popularly known as "the English Sappho", Darby Robinson embraced the natural eroticism of the female body in her work. Her voice was brave and sensual, and still speaks to the young readers of today. The following poem portrays a passionate admiration for earth's satellite.

Ode to the Moon

Pale Goddess of the witching hour;
Blest Contemplation's placid friend;
Oft in my solitary bow'r,
I mark thy lucid beam
From thy crystal car descend,
Whitening the spangled heath, and limpid sapphire stream.

And oft, amidst the shades of night
I court thy undulating light;
When Fairies dance around the verdant ring,
Or frisk beside the bubbling spring,

When the thoughtless shepherd's song
Echoes thro' the silent air,
As he pens his fleecy care,
Or plods with saunt'ring gait, the dewy meads along.

Chaste Orb! as thro' the vaulted sky
Feath'ry clouds transparent sail;
When thy languid, weeping eye,
Sheds its soft tears upon the painted vale;
As I ponder o'er the floods,
Or tread with listless step, th'embow'ring woods,
O, let thy transitory beam,
Soothe my sad mind, with fancy's aëry dream.

Wrapt in reflection let me trace
O'er the vast ethereal space,
Stars, whose twinkling fires illume
Dark-brow'd night's obtrusive gloom;
Where across the concave wide;
Flaming meteors swiftly glide;
Or along the milky way,
Vapours shoot a silvery ray;
And as I mark, thy faint reclining head,
Sinking on Ocean's pearly bed;
Let reason tell my soul, thus all things fade.

The Seasons change, the "garish sun"
When Day's burning car hath run
Its fiery course, no more we view,
While o'er the mountain's golden head,
Streak'd with tints of crimson hue,
Twilight's filmy curtains spread,
Stealing o'er Nature's face, a desolating shade.

Yon musky flow'r, that scents the earth;
The sod, that gave its odours birth;
The rock, that breaks the torrent's force;
The vale, that owns its wand'ring course;
The woodlands where the vocal throng
Trill the wild melodious song;
Thirsty desarts, sands that glow,
Mountains, cap'd with flaky snow;
Luxuriant groves, enamell'd fields,
All, all, prolific Nature yields,
Alike shall end; the sensate heart,
With all its passions, all its fire,
Touch'd by fate's unerring dart,
Shall feel its vital strength expire;
Those eyes, that beam with friendship's ray,
And glance ineffable delight,
Shall shrink from life's translucid day,
And close their fainting orbs, in death's impervious night.

Then what remains for mortal pow'r;
But time's dull journey to beguile;
To deck with joy, the winged hour,
To meet its sorrows with a patient smile;
And when the toilsome pilgrimage shall end,
To greet the tyrant, as a welcome friend.

FELICIA DOROTHEA HEMANS
1793-1835

Influenced by Williams Wordsworth and Lord Byron, Felicia Dorothea Hemans gained most of her knowledge from her father's grand library. Homeschooled by her mother and learned in several languages, Felicia Dorothea Hemans published nineteen volumes of poetry throughout her lifetime. Her popularity within the poetic world did not rightly represent her inner world, which was filled with separation, distress, and frail health. The following poem directly addresses the moon as the source of the poet's inspiration. The speaker begs for its influence, it's "soft music" and "heavenly airs", to shine down on her.

Moon-Light

Come, gentle muse! now all is calm,
The dew descends, the air is balm;
Unruffled is the glassy deep,
While moon-beams o'er its bosom sleep;
The gale of summer mildly blows,
The wave in soothing murmur flows;
Unclouded Vesper shines on high,
And ev'ry flow'r has clos'd its tearful eye.

Oh! at this hour, this placid hour,
Soft music, wake thy magic pow'r!
Be mine to hear thy dulcet measure,
Thy warbling strains, that whisper, pleasure;
Thy heavenly airs, of cadence dying,
And harp to every zephyr sighing;
When roving by the shadowy beam,
That gilds the fairy-bow'r and woodland-stream!

But all is still! no mellow sound
Floats on the breeze of night around;
Yet fancy, with some airy spell,
Can wake 'sweet Echo' from her cell;
Can charm her pensive votary's ear,
With plaintive numbers melting near;
And bid celestial spirits rise,
To pour their wild, enchanted melodies.

I love the rosy dawn of day,
When Zephyr wakes the laughing May;
I love the summer-evening's close,
That lulls the mind in calm repose;
But sweeter far the hour serene,
When softer colours paint the scene;
When Vesper sheds a dewy ray,
And o'er the sleeping wave the moon-beams play.

GERTRUDE STEIN
1874-1946

Born to an upper-class family in Allegheny, Pennsylvania, Gertrude Stein moved to Vienna as a young child. Then, after her parents death, she moved back to the United States, to Baltimore, and studied at Radcliffe College. Those who taught her believed deeply in her skills, and she was urged to attend medical school at Johns Hopkins University. After an unsuccessful tenure, she delivered the controversial speech "The Value of College Education for Women." 2014 marked the one hundred year anniversary for her groundbreaking modernist collection, TENDER BUTTONS. The following poem, from that collection, combines sex, desire, politics, and feminism in an ambiguous marriage of image and meaning. Read Stein once, then read her again.

A Light in the Moon

A light in the moon the only light is on Sunday. What was the sensible decision. The sensible decision was that notwithstanding many declarations and more music, not even notwithstanding the choice and a torch and a collection, notwithstanding the celebrating hat and a vacation and even more noise than cutting, notwithstanding Europe and Asia and being overbearing, not even notwithstanding an elephant and a strict occasion, not even withstanding more cultivation and some seasoning, not even with drowning and with the ocean being encircling, not even with more likeness and any cloud, not even with terrific sacrifice of pedestrianism and a special resolution, not even more likely to be pleasing. The care with which the rain is wrong and the green is wrong and the white is wrong, the care with which there is a chair and plenty of breathing. The care with which there is incredible justice and likeness, all this makes a magnificent asparagus, and also a fountain.

FINIS

From Stein to Finch to Sappho, we bid you farewell, but not for long, dear reader, for the voices of these women are still speaking. For now though, we are ever so grateful for your reading.

ABOUT THE AUTHOR

(Photo credit: Chris Jetté)

Abriana Jetté is an internationally published poet, essayist, and educator. Her work has appeared in dozens of journals, including the *Dr. T. J. Eckleburg Review*, *The Iron Horse Literary Review*, *The American Literary Review*, and *The Moth*. She teaches at St. Johns's University and the City University of New York, writes a regular column for *Stay Thirsty Magazine* that focuses on emerging poets and is the editor of the recently published book, *The Best Emerging Poets of 2013*, that debuted on Amazon as the #3 Best Seller in Poetry Anthologies. She lives in Brooklyn, New York.

CPSIA information can be obtained
at www.ICGtesting.com
Printed in the USA
FFHW012226090319
50978017-56401FF